# Pink House Living

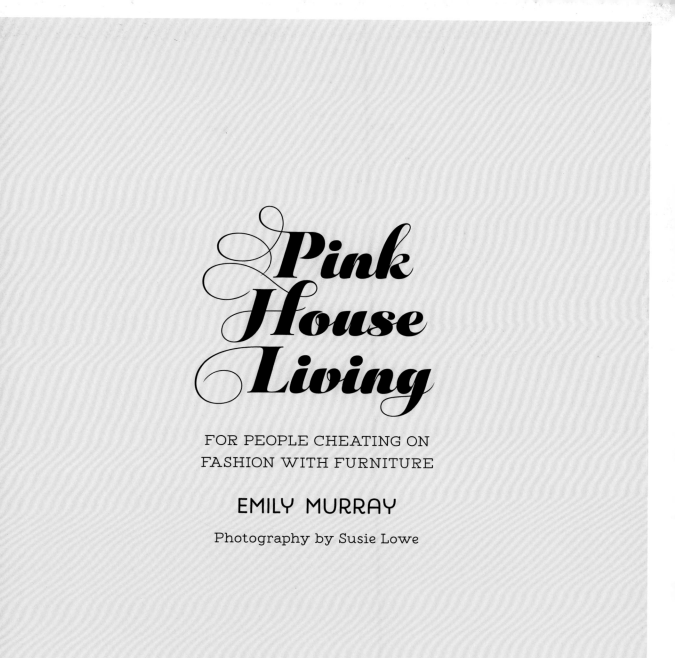

# Pink House Living

## FOR PEOPLE CHEATING ON FASHION WITH FURNITURE

### EMILY MURRAY

Photography by Susie Lowe

RYLAND PETERS & SMALL
LONDON • NEW YORK

SENIOR DESIGNER  Toni Kay
SENIOR COMMISSIONING EDITOR
  Annabel Morgan
PRODUCTION MANAGER
  Gordana Simakovic
ART DIRECTOR  Leslie Harrington
EDITORIAL DIRECTOR  Julia Charles
PUBLISHER  Cindy Richards

First published in 2019 by
Ryland Peters & Small
20-21 Jockey's Fields,
London WC1R 4BW
and
341 East 116th Street
New York, NY 10029

www.rylandpeters.com

Text and photographs copyright
© Emily Murray 2019
Design copyright © Ryland Peters
& Small 2019

10 9 8 7 6 5 4 3 2 1

ISBN 978-1-78879-084-0

A CIP record for this book is
available from the British Library.

Library of Congress CIP data has
been applied for.

Printed and bound in China

# Contents

# *Introduction* Why Pink?

When I came up with The Pink House as a name for my blog, and @pinkhouseliving for my Instagram account, I didn't think I'd spend much time talking about pink. Pink was MY favourite colour, sure, but I was using 'pink' as a proxy for ANY colour – for my readers' favourite colour, perhaps. I simply found a name that resonated for me and hoped others would find their own interpretation. But I'd underestimated the power of pink.

It turns out that pink is incredibly popular, on every level and in every way. We love pink. We love it on front doors, on walls and on rugs. We love it on Instagram, in magazines and in fabric charts. We love it in barely there blush, fuchsia and neon. And we love it in spite of – and sometimes because of – our partners' aversion to it. Pink House Husband, I'm looking at you.

But don't make the mistake of thinking that pink is just for girls. Not any more it isn't. And back in Victorian times it wasn't, when pink was a colour often used to dress baby boys, as it was seen as a paler form of red, which stood for power and masculinity. Funnily enough, blue – perceived as a softer, more gentle colour – was for the female of the species. In our more enlightened times, when girls can be boxing, biophysicist bad-asses, and boys are free(er) to work flexibly, design fashion and file their nails, the idea that certain colours – or jobs, character traits or sports – 'belong' to certain genders is increasingly

absurd. For more on this, I'd recommend Scarlett Curtis's collection of essays, *Feminists Don't Wear Pink (and other lies)*.

So yes, pink is for people, but it's also the colour of freedom, of individuality, of change. It's the colour of anti-Trump pussy hats, gay rights movements and breast cancer charities, all of which use pink to add power to their campaigns.

It's for all these reasons, plus the fact that I was simply BORN loving pink (despite my mother's aversion to it and the absence of pink princess dresses among the Oxfam hand-me-downs I wore as a kid), that this lighter shade of red has always and unwaveringly been my favourite colour. Even during my teenage goth years. Although I was a rubbish goth – too optimistic. And too pink.

So it's not surprising that pink is usually the colour at the front of my mind when I'm designing a room. That doesn't mean I like all my rooms dressed in floor-to-ceiling fuchsia though. Even when I have free rein to decorate exactly as I choose, without the Pink House Husband power of veto (as with my Home Office – see p.132), I exercise pink restraint. For me, the key to making the most of this joyous colour – for I fully believe that pink has an amazing power to make people happy – is using it in moderation. Of course, sometimes moderation should be used in moderation too – if you've ever experienced the pinkwash joys of places like London's Sketch (see p.58) or Pietro Nolita in New York, you'll know what I mean.

I discovered the joy of decorating – with pink, and other happy-making hues – after having a baby left me swathed in shapeless black leggings, sitting in an off-white room with my tyrannical offspring attached to one greyish breast. My collection of brightly coloured, two-sizes-too-small party dresses now belonged to another life (and another owner, via a charity shop/thrift store clear-out). There was less chance of me sipping jewel-hued cocktails in fabulous bars than there was of *Sex and the City*'s Samantha settling down. No wonder I started cheating on fashion with furniture. Well, if it was good enough for Carrie Bradshaw...

As I take you now on a guided tour through the rooms I've designed in my former house in Edinburgh, and my new one in South London, you'll see that pink is always present in various forms, from the palest neutral blush to hot pink neon, but I've tried to be careful with how I use it. Sometimes this is to take Pink House Husband's desires into consideration (though I will state for the record that too much compromise in interior design is never a good thing – I'll therefore be offering up my tips on winning the interior war as we go along); sometimes the better to accentuate a particular architectural feature, piece of furniture or artwork. And sometimes simply to allow another gorgeous colour to shine.

As well as sharing my decor mistakes, triumphs and learnings from the rooms I've designed, I'll be interviewing some of the interior gurus who have inspired me along the way, and showcasing some of the incredible spaces they've created.

So, what are we waiting for? The kettle's on; rosé's chilling in the fridge – welcome to The Pink House!

# *Quiz* ARE YOU CHEATING ON FASHION WITH FURNITURE?

Following the gestation and ejection of two children, clothes don't look quite as good on me as they once did. Add to this the fact that the same children have seriously curtailed my cocktails-with- the-girls nights out, and my life's looking less *Sex and the City*, and more Sofa and Sit-y (and Clothes that don't Fit-y). So, little by little, I've stopped being seduced by shoes and started flirting with soft furnishings instead – a velvet armchair doesn't care about the size of your feet or waistline, and it's great for cuddling up to while watching the latest box set. Yep, however I might try to hide it under last season's smock dress and some manky Stan Smiths, I'm being unfaithful to fashion with furniture. But what about you? Are you similarly smitten by all things home decor? Or will fashion always be your first love? Take my failsafe quiz to find out…

## 1  WHICH OF THESE WOMEN WOULD YOU MOST LIKE TO BE?

A) Kelly Wearstler
B) Cameron Diaz
C) Carrie Bradshaw
D) Anna Wintour

## 2  WHAT'S YOUR IDEA OF A GREAT NIGHT OUT?

A) Out? Why would I want to go out?
B) That beautiful new restaurant designed by Philippe Starck. If the babysitter doesn't cancel again.
C) Somewhere my dress matches the wallpaper.
D) New York's garment district, darling.

## 3  WHAT ARE YOUR VIEWS ON FIDELITY?

A) Is that a new fabric range from Liberty? What are the colourways?
B) As long as it looks like I'm being faithful, that's good enough for me.
C) I'm definitely into it. But you can be faithful to lots of people, right?
D) Till death do us party.

## 4  WHO IS YOUR FAVOURITE HANDBAG DESIGNER?

A) I use a plastic bag these days.
B) Does Jonathan Adler do bags?
C) Oh, I just love anything by Céline.
D) Those new-season Gucci bags are stunning!

## 5  DESCRIBE WHAT'S ON YOUR SOFA RIGHT NOW

A) You mean my new velvet sofa chaise? Well, I've banned the children from even looking at it, and styled it up with some designer cushions.
B) I'm getting my vintage chesterfield reupholstered in a Missoni fabric, so there's nothing on it right now.
C) My lovely, squashy corner sofa is strewn with my latest shopping purchases – I'm trying to decide what to wear for date night…
D) I think I sold my sofa to pay for that Pucci dress. Let me just check…

## 6  HOW DO YOU DRESS YOUR CHILDREN?

A) In anything that won't stain the posh new sofa.
B) In nice clothes that look cute photographed against the freshly painted walls.
C) In H&M and a bit of Stella McCartney. Like me.
D) I like the hipster basics. And a touch of classic Parisian cool. And I'm always checking Instagram for the hottest new kidswear labels…

## 7  WHAT HASHTAG ARE YOU MOST LIKELY TO USE ON INSTAGRAM?

A) #decoraddict
B) #colourmyhome
C) #sohotrightnow
D) #ootd

## 8  STAND IN YOUR LIVING ROOM AND LOOK DOWN AT YOUR FEET. WHAT'S YOUR FIRST THOUGHT?

A) Doesn't my new rug set off the reclaimed floorboards beautifully!
B) The pattern on my old Nikes would look amazing on a dinner service.
C) Ooh, look how my velvet slippers go perfectly with the new carpet.
D) I only bought these Louboutins last week, but they're looking a little tired already – it might be time for a new pair of heels…better sell the fridge…

### MOSTLY As:

You've chucked out your Choos, your fashion fund has become cushion money and in place of a wardrobe/armoire you've installed a velvet chaise longue. You're not just cheating on clothes with furniture; you're a brazen hussy when it comes to your home. And we're proud of you!

### MOSTLY Bs:

Yes, you have a cute Stella McCartney dress – but isn't that from, like, eight seasons ago? You're trying to keep up fashion appearances – and succeeding for the most part – but the truth is your love of fabulous patterns, colours and fabrics has transferred to your home. Your wardrobe might have suffered, but at least your living room looks lovely.

### MOSTLY Cs:

When you go out, you're the same super-stylish lady you were five years ago, even if you now go out once every five weeks, instead of five times in one week. But the drastic change in your life is that you're now in a polygamous relationship – you've discovered the delights of home decor, so now you're sharing the love between fashion and furniture. How very modern!

### MOSTLY Ds:

You made your wedding vows to fashion, and you have no intention of breaking them for the latest sexy sofa. You agreed to stand by your man, and that man is Marc Jacobs, not Jonathan Adler. Wallpaper, reclaimed wooden floors and soft furnishings come and go, but Louboutins are for life. At least until they get a bit scuffed, anyway.

# 1

# The Exterior & Hallway

The Pink House blog wasn't just inspired by my passion for pink. It was also named after my actual house in Edinburgh, which I painted pink (specifically, Farrow & Ball's dusky Cinder Rose) on the outside. When we moved into the multi-coloured street of listed Arts and Crafts terraced houses, however, ours was the only property painted white. The other houses sported pretty shades of periwinkle blue, burnt ochre and moss green…but no pink.

# The Exterior

**OPPOSITE** I painted my London front door in Farrow & Ball's Nancy's Blushes, which goes beautifully with the brass letterbox and knocker and bespoke brass plaque.

In my desire to swiftly remedy the white house situation, I chose the colour I knew the husband would be most likely to agree to: green. And agree he did. It was only then that I realized I didn't want a green house. I wanted a pretty house. I wanted a PINK house.

'Not a chance,' was Pink House Husband's response. 'Anyway, the neighbours wouldn't be up for it.' This gave me an idea. I wrote a short letter to each of our 14 new neighbours explaining that we were planning to paint our house either green or pink, and did they have a preference? The response: two-thirds green, one-third pink (innovation is never easy). I reported the results faithfully to my life partner: 'Two-thirds of our neighbours say they'd prefer us to paint it pink. We shouldn't upset them when we've only just arrived.' Incredibly, Pink House Husband bought it (I think he was having a busy week at work), and I wasted no time in buying the paint.

Another aspect that helped me push through the pink house concept was the front door colour: charcoal grey (Farrow & Ball's Railings). This would, I explained, prevent the pink from looking too pretty-pretty and ensure everything remained 'grounded' (a good, solid, masculine word). Plus, it looks lush with the brass door furniture. Dark grey and pale pink was, and remains, one of my favourite colour combinations. Once the pink paint was applied and the very serious door given its final touches, the ever-cheery Pink House Husband admitted: 'It's not TOO awful.' Which means he loved it.

Moving to our red-brick Edwardian South London home meant saying goodbye to a pink exterior – or did it? I researched rendering, with a view to rose-tinting the render, but Pink House Husband made it abundantly clear that this was not an option. And you've got to pick your battles, right? After all, I had a whole house to renovate – I didn't want to use up all my pink credits before I'd even crossed the threshold.

At least I still had the front door. And grudging permission to paint it. But what shade would work against the brick? I've always found red and pink to be a challenging combination. In fact, I don't knowingly have any red decor in my home. But that's not to say pink and red is a mistake – far from it.

For me, the orangey red of my brickwork was best accompanied by a more muted pink with slightly peachy notes (Nancy's Blushes from Farrow & Ball). But a word of warning when it comes to exterior paints: make sure you properly test how the colour will read outside, as the brighter light means it will seem like a different shade compared to indoors – paler and less intense.

Now that the front door is pink, I'm keen to paint windows and woodwork/trim to match. And perhaps grow some pink roses around the door. Maybe I'll add a few window boxes too – cyclamen, petunias, fuchsia, busy lizzies and geraniums all work well in window boxes and, crucially, come in umpteen shades of pink. Who says you need render to get the pink house party started?

# Pinkspiration

Fashion and lifestyle photographer Victoria Metaxas (@victoriametaxas) travels the world in search of colourful locations for her shoots. Who better to ask about the perfect pink house and the world's best places to ogle colourful exteriors?

**Q** What attracts you to colourful exteriors?

**A** They put a smile on my face! Colourful houses bring happiness and add positivity to a street. I always wonder who lives behind which door and why they chose that particular colour for their house. I respect pink house owners for painting their home such a bold, bright hue.

**Q** What is it about pink you love so much?

**A** Seeing anything pink puts a spring in my step – it's such a joyful colour. I also love that it represents femininity; I'm an unashamedlygirlie girl.

**Q** Which is your favourite of all the pink houses you've photographed?

**A** Oh, that is a very tough question! In London, the light pink house with a grey door on Uxbridge Street (see opposite). With its pink flowers in the window, light grey door and fence, and white-edged windows, it's a perfect example of pink elegance.

**Q** What shade of pink looks best on a house exterior or door?

**A** I find dusty pinks work best on a house – it's fun yet still elegant. Candy pink can look a little too twee for my taste, and baby pink seems too girlie.

**Q** What colour door goes best with a pink house?

**A** I would say a white or grey door; I like to keep things classic.

**Q** And what colour house looks best with a pink door?

**A** I think you could get away with a beautiful sage or mint green with a dusty pink door. For a bright pink door, I'd stick with white to ensure the door gets all the attention.

**Q** Which country or city has the best stock of coloured houses?

**A** In no particular order I would say: Lisbon, Portugal – the colourful tiles and buildings are a match made in heaven. Next, Burano, Italy – I visited Burano last year and fell in love. The colours are as vibrant as you see in photos. The Cinque Terre, also in Italy, are outstanding. To be honest, the entire Italian Riviera is a colour-lovers' paradise. Finally, Copenhagen is stunning. The Nyhavn is particularly amazing and well worth a visit.

**Q** Has society's attitude to pink changed in recent years?

**A** We increasingly live in a world where women can love pink – a colour that still represents femininity – and still be perceived as strong and powerful. I love that beautiful contrast and what it signifies for our generation.

# The Hallway

I love to make an entrance. Which is why it's important that my home does the same. Even if you're not a show-off like me, your home's entrance matters too.

The hallway is the first impression guests get of your home's interior, so this is your chance to set the scene. More importantly, it's the first welcome YOU get when arriving home, so you want it to be a good one.

What was the first impression I wanted people to have of my Edinburgh home? PINK! But this wasn't quite as straightforward as it sounds. I might have got a pink exterior past the not-so-vigilant Pink House Husband, but an entirely pink hallway and two flights of stairs? This was going to be tricky. Want to know how I won this particular interior war? Here we go then...

Firstly, I did not say, 'I want to paint the hallway pink.' Instead, I chose a shade of Farrow & Ball pink similar to the shade I was planning to use, and gave it its proper name: Setting Plaster. 'Plaster' has a nice DIY feel to it (Pink House Husband loves a bit of DIY), and I stressed that it was a 'rich, warm colour' that would 'go well with the woodwork'. Funnily enough, he had no objections.

Although he had agreed to Setting Plaster, this wasn't my final colour destination. The colour I was after was Farrow & Ball's Pink Ground, which is lighter and, well, pinker than Setting Plaster. Annoyingly, it also has the word 'Pink' in the title, meaning I'd been unable to refer to it directly by name in the first instance. But I had a plan. I bought sample/tester pots of both Setting Plaster and Pink Ground, and painted sections of the hallway in Pink Ground ONLY.

'What do you think?' I asked Pink House Husband. Assuming it was the manly Setting Plaster, he condoned it with barely a glance. A little later I painted sections of Setting Plaster alongside the Pink Ground. When he emerged from his office I said, casually: 'I tried this darker one too, but I think it's just too brown, don't you?' He agreed. Voila! One pink hallway, and I didn't even have to bend the truth.

It must have been around this time that Pink House Husband stopped having so many interior design opinions. I don't know how else to explain him agreeing to my papering the basement hallway in Cole & Son's rainbow-hued Prism wallpaper (a wallcovering so wonderful I had to hang it in my house somewhere). Actually I do: I just didn't tell him. This is not usually a strategy I'd recommend, as it can prove expensive, not just in terms of repapering but also the divorce lawyer. In this instance, I'm happy to report that both the walls and the marriage remained intact.

The Alternative Flooring polka-dot stair carpet and brass stair rods were the last things I added to my Edinburgh home before we moved to London (I fitted this carpet to two flights of stairs and a landing, then moved house three months later. Yes, it was emotional). I've never understood why stair carpets have to be plain; patterns are great at hiding the dirt, and if your stairs make you smile, you'll be happy through all the ups and downs.

The soft pink walls
provide a contrast to
the large, vibrant oil
painting by graffiti-
turned-fine-artist
Dale vN Marshall. If
we'd stayed longer in
the Edinburgh house,
my next task would
have been to paint
the spindles.

# Pinkspiration

This bubblegum-pink eight-storey stairwell is an installation by Simon Whybray called 'hi boo I love you', imagined as a love letter to his fiancée (they are now happily married – it worked!). Its home is a former multi-storey car park in Peckham, South London, part of not-for-profit Bold Tendencies' collection of site-specific art and cultural events. I chatted to the organization's Charlie Mills and Sofia Benitez (@boldtendencies).

**Q** How did the stairwell look before Simon's installation?

**A** When Bold Tendencies took over the old multi-storey car park, the stairwell hadn't seen much action since the Sainsbury's supermarket closed in 1993. It was mucky and the walls were covered in a 1980s beige-yellow paint with flecks of brown.

**Q** What made you decide to transform the stairs into a work of art?

**A** We wanted our visitors to feel welcome as soon as they crossed the threshold. There are restrictions regarding what you can install when it comes to a functioning staircase, but Simon's idea was impactful and immersive while remaining faithful to the fabric of the building.

**Q** This staircase has become a cult Instagram hit. Why do you think it has been so popular?

**A** When we commissioned 'hi boo', no one knew how much it would blow up on Instagram. But pink seems to have this weird currency on social media platforms that makes people want to replicate it; to share it. Pink has become synonymous online with youth and wealth – and even innocence.

**Q** This colour looks like Baker-Miller Pink - the pink that's supposed to soothe criminals. Is it?

**A** This isn't intended to be Baker-Miller Pink, but colour is so culturally fluid that every year since the stairwell was painted in 2016 people have come up with different associations. We don't think this stairwell is especially soothing – instead, people enter and get a buzz. They can't stop talking about it!

**Q** How do you think society's perception of pink has changed in recent times?

**A** We recently went to a show called 'The Politics of Pink' that investigated whether pink had become gender neutral. We don't think it has; we're still culturally conditioned to see pink and blue as girls' and boys' colours respectively. But the more certain images gain power online, the more colours – including pink – take on new meanings and associations.

# 2

# The Kitchen

I was faced with the same problem in each kitchen I inherited in my Edinburgh and London houses: it looked too much like a kitchen. Each room was almost sterile in its unembellished kitchen-ness. Even allowing for the total tidy-up that precedes a house sale, these two kitchens were majorly lacking in personality before I started renovating.

In my north-facing Edinburgh kitchen, there were white laminate cabinets, black granite worktops, whitewashed walls, black stone tiles on the floor and a strip of spotlights that made the room so bright that the absence – or presence – of sunlight outside was irrelevant. In London, the cabinets were at least a colour – teal – but the work surface was an unrelenting white composite, the walls a light beige and the cabinet handles and mixer tap/faucet what I described as institutional chrome.

Increasingly, we live in open-plan homes, with kitchens connected to dining areas and even living spaces. As well as feeling sterile, personality-free kitchens are, in my view, a waste of an opportunity to create a colourful room that makes you happy. And open-plan 'kitcheny' kitchens also create a disconnect from the rooms they adjoin. In both my kitchens I considered the space as a whole, with my main aim being to design a kitchen that appeared to be an extension of the room alongside it.

**RIGHT** As one of the first rooms I renovated, my Edinburgh open-plan kitchen was light on pink, as I was still working out how to get the colour approved by the pink-sceptic Pink House Husband.

In Edinburgh, this was the family living area, so I started by painting both sides of the room in the same strong mid-grey shade (Manor House Gray by Farrow & Ball) with the woodwork/trim coated in a creamy white (White Tie, again by Farrow & Ball). But what of the slightly grubby laminate cabinets? Essentially, I wanted the floor cabinets to be dark and the wall-mounted cabinets to be pale so that they seemed less heavy. I was keen to keep the black granite work surface, and I wanted the whole effect to be that of a bespoke kitchen that had been pieced together. And I needed some bling, in the form of heavy brass Buster + Punch handles.

I loved the matt finish of my Edinburgh cabinets so much that I wanted to replicate the effect in my next kitchen. My starting point for the London kitchen was a leafy green and pink wallpaper to connect the space to the outside; the bifold doors and the nature reserve beyond our garden gate mean the room feels very close to nature. I decided to hang the wallpaper before making any other decorating decisions so that we could get a feel for how this one big change affected the other elements of the space – something I'd really recommend.

As it turned out, the green in the wallpaper helped bring out the green in the cabinets, and by adding a brighter shade of green via the zig-zag tile, I created the indoor forest effect I'd been after. The wallpaper also appeared darker than I'd expected – it has a black background after all – so painting the cabinets dark would have been too much anyway.

A final word on my decision to replace the white composite work surface in my London kitchen with Carrara marble. When I first mentioned this on Instagram, I was deluged with messages telling me I was insane: marble

**OPPOSITE** These gold counter stools from Bend Goods add a luxe look to the kitchen and work perfectly with the brass tap, handles and clock.

**ABOVE TOP** Adding high-end handles to existing cabinet doors is much cheaper than ripping the whole kitchen out and starting all over again.

**ABOVE** This is a Minoan sink mixer tap/faucet with crosshead handles in polished brass from Perrin & Rowe.

**PAGES 38-39** Get creative with tiles to make a statement in your kitchen. These green encaustic cement Alalpardo tiles from Bert & May can be arranged in many different patterns. The pink tiled breakfast bar with brass trim looks lovely alongside gold Bend Goods counter stools.

**LEFT** Incorporating a reading nook in the kitchen adds to the laid-back vibe. The armchair is from Sofas & Stuff, upholstered in Ian Mankin Velvet Airforce. The pink silk bird cushion is by Mariska Meijers.

**OPPOSITE** The woodwork/trim around the windows is painted Farrow & Ball Calamine. The soft pink complements the Carrara marble worktop and ties in with the flowery black Malin wallpaper by Sandberg.

was porous, stained easily and would be wrecked in no time, I was told. But I loved the idea of having a stunning slab of natural material in the middle of my home and decided to go for it anyway.

A week after it was installed, I had a huge 40th birthday party at home and the marble breakfast bar played host to 40 bottles of pink champagne. The next morning, there were bottle rings all over the surface (they come up as a different texture, not a different colour, so you only see the marks when the light hits them at a certain angle). But you know what? I love them! They're a permanent (unless I decide to repolish the surface) reminder of an amazing night with rivers of posh pink fizz. Plus they're part of the patina of family life. Bring on those fun-time stains, I say!

# HOW TO CREATE A NON-KITCHENY KITCHEN

**ASYMMETRY** In my Edinburgh kitchen I used the same T-bar handles on the lower cabinets and drawers, but fitted them differently (vertically on cabinets, horizontally on drawers) for a custom-made effect.

**BOOKS** A shelf of books in the kitchen humanizes the space – and they don't need to be recipe books either. I like keeping a pretty selection of vintage fiction kicking around my kitchen.

**MATT SURFACES** Too many reflective surfaces – be they tiles, laminate cabinets or chrome appliances – can feel harsh and unfriendly. Step away from the shine by using natural finishes such as wooden flooring and painting laminate with matt-finish paint.

**ART** You might not feel comfortable hanging heirloom works of art in the kitchen, but framed inexpensive prints or even family photos arranged as a gallery wall (see p.57) look great.

**PLANTS** A kitchen is a great place to have plants – they add life to a utilitarian environment and it's (theoretically) easy to keep them alive due to the close proximity of water. If your fingers are more pink than green, don't be ashamed to go faux – there are so many super-realistic fakes out there nowadays.

**TEXTILES** I'm talking rugs and tea/dish towels here. You'd be amazed by how much DOESN'T get spilled on a kitchen rug – choose a patterned, inexpensive, machine-washable number (mine was from Anthropologie, which has a great selection) and it'll add a slightly decadent warmth to your kitchen space. And tea/dish towels are basically cheap art for your oven door, so have some fun!

**COLOUR** In an open-plan kitchen, using the same colour – or wallpaper - on the walls of the adjoining room gives the sense of a larger living space, especially if you follow my tips above.

# Pinkspiration

Sarah Akwisombe (@sarahakwisombe) is an award-winning interiors blogger and stylist who's all about doing things differently. She was commissioned by a client to create this apartment in Southend-on-Sea for the Airbnb market, with a brief to make it 'as Instagrammable as possible' on a very tight budget.

**Q** How did you want the room to feel when it was finished?

**A** Like a space for Millennials; somewhere kitsch and fun. Millennial pink was the obvious choice, but I actually went for more of a peachy pink tone that created a 1950s vibe when paired with the tomato red velvet sofa. The flooring added a bit of drama and the neon sign the fun.

**Q** Why did you decide to use pink as part of the scheme?

**A** This space wasn't about being ahead of the trends or trying to be too clever or serious; it was about capturing the zeitgeist and for me that is just PINK. I also knew it would have instant impact and be an attention grabber on Instagram.

**Q** If someone is designing a kitchen from scratch, where would you advise them to start?

**A** I think with the layout really. Much as I hate myself for saying this, kitchens are all about practicality. Then you can work in one statement-making element – maybe a cool tile, a brightly coloured tap/faucet or an unusual work surface

**Q** Any tips on creating a kid-friendly kitchen?

**A** Use scrubbable paint! Also, my daughter loves to be involved with the cooking, so think about storage space for a little footstool. And induction hobs/cooktops are great because they are so safe for kids. Even if you put your hand on the hob/cooktop, you won't feel any heat unless you're a magnetic pan.

**Q** What kind of statement do you think pink makes in home decor?

**A** I think pink is a super-versatile colour. So the statement could be 'I'm cool and sophisticated' or 'I'm kitsch and loud' depending on the shade. I love to use this very vivid, almost lipstick pink. It's the shade I have on the ceiling in my living room and it always creeps into the branding for my business too. You can't simply say 'I don't like pink' (like so many men do!) because I really think there is a shade for everyone. (See p.139 to find out which shade of pink is right for you.)

# 3

# The Dining Room

Before the kids came along, the Pink House Husband and I were living carefree, wine-saturated lives in a flat in Archway, north London. Yes, the area was a bit rough around the edges, but that was part of its appeal. We loved sauntering home under unsavoury canal bridges, passing suspect persons doing god-knows-what in the shadows. No sanitized suburbs for us thank you very much! Then guess what? Yep, we had a baby and 10 months later, to save our sanity, had swapped the squalor of the Big Smoke for the manicured Range Rovers of south Edinburgh, where my parents (AKA free childcare) just happened to live.

Despite its bijou size, I'd already decided that the dining room in our Edinburgh house would be the place where we'd party with other grown-ups in the one-hour window between getting the kids into bed and passing out with exhaustion. I wanted this room to reflect our pre-kids, London-dwelling, much-cooler selves, and found just the wallpaper for this: Timorous Beasties' London Toile. As it was the Noughties, until this point I'd only ever used wallpaper in feature-wall fashion. But if I was going to let my party-girl side shine through, this wallpaper, with its pictures of people being mugged and getting smashed on park benches, should be pasted on EVERY SINGLE WALL! My mother, needless to say, thought I was mad.

And then, of course, seven years later we moved back to this wonderful, crazy city. So what to do with our new dining room? The London dining room is open to the family room and kitchen, and leads directly to the garden via glass doors, so the obvious choice was a continuation of the kitchen's leafy wallpaper.

In contrast to my Edinburgh dining room, which was all about escaping the kids, this space is where all four of us spend most of our time when we're at home. A big, robust table was a must, and I unearthed this beautifully

**ABOVE** I hung these Paperchase baubles on the chandelier one Christmas and liked them so much that I left them there until we moved house three years later!

**RIGHT** A vintage light switch contrasts pleasingly with a scene from the Timorous Beasties London Toile wallpaper featuring the Gherkin building.

**OPPOSITE** This bird lamp is the cause of much controversy between me and the Pink House Husband: I love it; he doesn't. It started off here in the dining room, then migrated to my Home Office (see p.134) in our London house so that he didn't have to look at it any more.

patinated antique French table, complete with scorch marks, scratches and faint impressions of mathematical formulae from someone's long-forgotten homework. I never worry about the kids making marks on it– in fact, I like it when they do, as it adds to the table's story.

For seating options, I've assembled a motley crew comprising a vintage gym bench (reminder of my gymnastics days), Perspex Kartell Ghost chairs (brilliant for contrasting with solid furniture, as they don't take up much visual space), a gold chair to match the bar stools and a wicker hanging chair by the door (perfect for soaking up the sun in this south-facing space).

A gallery 'wall of words' behind the table and my work here is done. Although apparently everyone is 'starving hungry' now. Must be Deliveroo o'clock…

**PAGE 52** As a former gymnast, when I found this vintage gym bench at Retrouvius, I had to buy it immediately. Whenever possible, buy items that call out to you, even if you've no idea where they will go.

**PAGE 53** This wicker hanging chair is from House Curious, with cactus cushions from Silken Favours and Bluebellgray to make it extra comfy.

**OPPOSITE ABOVE** This fabulous flower arrangement by London-based florist Hayford & Rhodes combines real flowers with faux blossom stems to spectacular effect.

**OPPOSITE BELOW** Touches of gold give a glamorous vibe – I even swapped the existing light switches for brass beauties by Buster + Punch.

**ABOVE** This comfy nook links the dining area and kitchen – sometimes I sit on it to supervise the kids' dinner; sometimes to chat to the Pink House Husband while he makes soup.

## HOW TO CREATE
## A GALLERY WALL

**1** Choose a common
thread for the pictures:
this could be a colour,
style or imagery theme,
or just a group of
images or hangable
objects you love.

**2** Pick frames in one colour
or style for a more
unified look or to add
cohesion to an eclectic
picture selection.

**3** Measure the wall size on
the floor; lay out your
pictures on this floor
space until you've found
the best configuration.

**4** Take a photo of your
'gallery floor'.

**5** For extra precision,
measure the gaps
between the pictures.

**6** Starting centrally, hang
your pictures on the
wall one by one, using
the photo and/or
measurements for
guidance.

**LEFT** My gallery wall includes
a 24/7 print by We Are Amused;
papier mâché animal heads from
Anthropologie; an Honor Oak
Park location print by Octavia
Plum; and a palm tree print
from Print Club London.

# Pinkspiration

The Gallery at Sketch, in London's Mayfair, is one of the world's most Instagrammed restaurants and a pink icon. The Paris-based restaurant's designer India Mahdavi has been crowned the 'queen of colour' by *Architectural Digest*. I spoke to India to find out more about how this fabulous space – one of my all-time favourites – was conceived.

**Q** What brief were you given for designing The Gallery at Sketch?

**A** Mourad [Mourad Mazouz, Sketch's owner] wanted a modern brasserie, and of course I had to work around David Shrigley's requirements: drawings on all the walls, white tabletops for tableware he had designed specially. The only constraint was to keep the floor, a mix of marbles and terrazzo conceived by Martin Creed.

**Q** What inspired you to design The Gallery using pink?

**A** When I initially visited The Gallery with Mourad, my first instinct was not only to create a strong contrast to Martin Creed's installation and to Sketch as a whole, but I also wanted a playful proposal for David Shrigley's work. Somehow, the idea of pink imposed itself; it was so obvious to me. The feminine pink could be treated in a radical modern way. Pink was the answer.

**Q** What did Mourad say when you told him of your plans to use pink?

**A** When I said, 'The place shall be pink!', Mourad told me, 'I don't like pink. But I trust you, so go ahead.' And it has now become the most Instagrammed restaurant in the world, and won several interior design awards.

**Q** Was it difficult deciding on the exact shade of pink? How would you describe the shade you used?

**A** The challenge was to find the right shade for a space that doesn't have any natural light. I described it as Hollywood pink because it gives a cinematographic feel to the room. But I wanted the essence of pink – not too yellow, not too blue.

**Q** Have you altered The Gallery's design now David Shrigley has replaced his monochrome drawings with colourful artworks?

**A** We reupholstered the furniture, as it needed freshening up, and changed the paint on the walls to a slightly darker pink to complement the new artworks.

**Q** Why has this room been such a hit on Instagram?

**A** I think because it was so radical to go monochrome and pink. Also, the place is really photogenic, and everybody looks good in it – with that three-day-tan glow!

**Q** If you had to redesign The Gallery in another single colour, which one would you choose?

**A** Mourad already asked me and I said I couldn't...

# 4

# The Sitting Room

A tale of two sitting rooms...

First of all, there was 'the den' in my Edinburgh basement. When we moved in, this was a relatively dark room with a low ceiling and small – but pretty – windows looking out onto the garden. I wanted to turn this unloved room into something that wouldn't look out of place in one of Kit Kemp's fabulous Firmdale Hotels. I wanted fabric walls, saturated colours, pattern clashes, loads of luxe and plenty of pink.

I started from scratch, ripping the room back to bare brick and hiring damp proofers, flooring specialists, plumbers, electricians, plasterers, carpenters and an interior designer, colour genius Jessica Buckley, to piece it back together. Walls were swathed in grasscloth. The floor was parquet. The cocktail bar was gold leaf and glass. I even had the neon sign made to order, the pink 'play' a copy of my own handwriting. So far, so swanky.

Then the soft furnishings arrived, all custom-upholstered. First the snugglers, in Osborne & Little velvet with pink velvet piping. And the sofa bed, dressed in Carnival by Christopher Farr. There was only one (large) problem: the sofa wouldn't fit down the stairs. AT ALL.

**PAGE 62** Firmdale Hotels' designer Kit Kemp is a big fan of this Carnival fabric from Christopher Farr; she uses it extensively in her Haymarket Hotel.

**ABOVE** My 'Ain't Nobody Got Time For That' cross-stitch cushion from Furbish Studio and the bespoke pink neon sign are two of my all-time favourite items of decor.

**OPPOSITE** I had hidden LED light strips fitted around the edge of this gold leaf cocktail bar to give it the impression of glowing from within. Inside the cabinet is a small fridge containing pink champagne (natch) and soft drinks.

**PAGES 66–67** Wall lights from Jim Lawrence were installed at both ends of the sofa bed so that they could double as bedside lamps when guests slept over; the lights can be switched off without leaving the bed. The coffee table is from West Elm and the op art by Bridget Riley.

But when you've spent thousands of pounds having a sofa upholstered, you find a way to fit it into your home. This was my way:

1 Enlist Pink House Husband, my mum, my engineer dad and his burly work colleagues to sort it out.

2 Run off to Marbella on a girls' holiday – and while I'm drinking prosecco in the sun, my crack team execute the following steps...

3 Remove dining room window.

4 Lower extremely expensive sofa out of window down to garden using ropes (Eek! Thank goodness I was in Marbs).

5 Discover basement hallway ceiling is too low to allow sofa to pivot into the room.

6 My mum unpicks the sofa's stitching, then Pink House Husband saws sofa into pieces using a hacksaw (there are no words).

7 Sofa pivots into room.

8 Pink House Husband bolts and glues sofa back together; my mum hand-stitches it back up.

9 I return home from Marbs, feeling refreshed.

And then we moved house – and the whole manoeuvre had to be reversed. You can imagine I wasn't the most popular person in my family that day. The moral of the story? ALWAYS measure your stairs and ceiling height before buying the sofa. And always scarper before the heavy lifting and sawing begins.

The sofas safely in my London sitting room, my aim was to turn this north-facing space into a cosy place for cuddling up in the evenings – but with a wow rock 'n' roll twist.

**OPPOSITE** Don't just consider colours when designing a room; shapes play a part too. Here, the round Sofas & Stuff velvet footstool references the Graham & Green pendant lamp, the sofa bed fabric and the gold circle in the Bowie print above the fireplace.

**ABOVE** I wanted this room's decor to highlight the original marble mantelpiece – the dark blue paint sets it off beautifully.

**PAGES 70–71** The room may be painted blue, but the focal points are all pink, including the alcoves, which are papered in a pale pink Designers Guild ombré cloud-effect wallcovering...all the better to show off my pink drinks collection. Special mention goes to the cabinet handles, which were custom-made by KOHR By Arsalan A. Khan from pink calcite and brass.

**OPPOSITE** One of my biggest interior design dislikes is harsh overhead lighting. So I remove bulbs from any central pendant lamps to prevent guests (or the husband) switching them on and instead add light from softer, peripheral sources such as this pink Pooky lamp and HAY wall candle sconce. Above the TV hangs a rowing blade I won with my college crew at university.

**ABOVE** This Emma J Shipley cushion ties in beautifully with my pink and blue snugglers. The gorgeous pink cheetahs reference the stylized leopard print Osborne & Little fabric.

Luckily the original fireplace was working, and ripping out the laminate floor revealed original floorboards just begging to be sanded. MDF alcove units fitted either side of the fireplace looked like they'd always been there after a lick of paint. The existing coving was plain and I wanted something fancier, so had Edwardian-era plaster cornicing/crown molding and a ceiling rose installed. This is surprisingly inexpensive and has a huge impact on the grandeur of the room.

As for the decor, I knew a deep rich blue paint – Farrow & Ball's Hague Blue – would set off the fabrics to perfection and hide the TV, while giving the room that after-dark cocktail vibe I was after. Everything else just fell into place: the Bowie art was begging to sit above the marble mantelpiece. An old corner cabinet was upcycled in green and gold by local experts Muck N Brass. Rose pink velvet curtains slid along a curved brass pole. Add a vintage Moroccan rug and a gold geometric pendant lamp and the room was ready for family films and post-dinner party cocktails.

And the sofa? You'd never guess what it's gone through.

**ABOVE RIGHT** Grouping together small bunches of flowers in little vases is a less formal approach to floristry and a great way to use those stems that break off larger bunches, or to display flowers from your garden.

**OPPOSITE** This corner drinks cabinet was given a new lease of life when I asked 'luxecycling' queen Zoe Pocock from Muck N Brass to work her magic with green and gold paint. Hot pink candles from W.A. Green brighten a dark corner.

## HOW TO STYLE NEON IN YOUR HOME

**1** Start with the neon – make that the focal point of the room, then work outwards from there.

**2** Think carefully about colour and the mood you're trying to create. For example, I used a soothing blue in the kids' rooms, and red in the kitchen for a party atmosphere.

**3** With customized designs, consider symbols or slogans that mean something special to you – tattoos and song lyrics are a good place to start (see p.140).

**4** If you work from home, add some neon to your workspace – perfect for those lightbulb moments!

**5** Don't be afraid to layer neon on top of prints or other art for that extra twist.

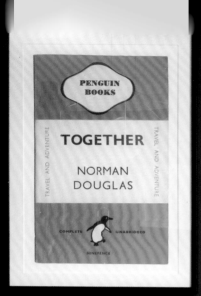

PENGUIN
BOOKS

TRAVEL AND ADVENTURE

TOGETHER

TRAVEL AND ADVENTURE

NORMAN
DOUGLAS

COMPLETE    UNABRIDGED

NINEPENCE

# Pinkspiration

Steven McGill designed this decadent sitting room for the Victorian apartment he shares with his partner Adrian in Glasgow's West End. Steven works in the travel industry, but is developing a new career as an interior designer (@stevenbellomcgill)

**Q** The pops of pink look amazing against navy walls. What made you decide to go dark in this room?

**A** This room is north facing – it was quite dark already, so I thought I'd go with that instead of fighting it. I like doing a contemporary take on Victorian colours – I've used Fired Earth's Carbon Blue on the walls and Farrow & Ball's Off-Black on the doors and skirting/baseboard to emphasize the outline.

**Q** You painted the window, ceiling and cornice/crown molding white – what was the thinking there?

**A** I usually paint rooms all one colour, but here I wanted to use a contrasting shade to draw the eye along the ceiling and down the window; it has a beautiful view onto a park.

**Q** Did you have a colour scheme and detailed design plan before you started decorating, or did you layer the design as you went along?

**A** I wanted to do justice to the building's history so I designed the sitting room around the original features, and used paint that referenced the deep colours that the Victorians used in their candlelit parlours. I already had the pink sofas and some amazing artworks, so they were all part of the plan too.

**Q** What led you to choose the Timorous Beasties fabrics on the sofa and armchairs?

**A** I was driving past the Timorous Beasties shop in Glasgow when I saw the armchairs – the explosion of colour was so amazing I nearly reversed back up the main road to get them! Then I found the Ercol sofa upholstered in the same fabric in the window at Bergdorf Goodman in New York. I couldn't believe it! When you see something you really love, you should just go for it.

**Q** What does pink mean to you?

**A** I think it's uplifting. Those sofas bring a burst of energy into the room. Pink can be soft and gentle, but it doesn't have to be feminine – it just depends on the context and the shade. And people's perceptions of the colour are changing – so many guys are wearing pink now...including me!

# 5

# The Family Room

This was one of the first rooms we renovated after moving into our Edinburgh house. As a result, I was still learning how to win the interior war against the husband (hence the lack of pink in this room). Its design also happened at a time when the kids were small, clingy and requiring constant attention. It soon became apparent that having a family room separate to the kitchen was a disaster. Instead of playing next door while I cooked (AKA heated stuff up – I'm no domestic goddess), my tiny progeny wanted to remain within touching distance of me; if I was in the kitchen, so were they, busily emptying drawers full of sharp/fragile objects. So we knocked a big hole in the wall between the family room and kitchen so that I could be rustling up dinner while they played wholesome games (watched TV) in plain sight of the sink.

**ABOVE** The room's colour scheme came from the James Hawkins painting over the mantelpiece, which I painted white to highlight this period feature against the grey walls.

Now that the kitchen was an extension of this south-facing space, we spent much more time in the family room. It just happened to be the best room in the house, with loads of original Victorian features, including a beautiful bay window with panelled shutters that let in tons of daylight.

Of course, the window didn't let in tons of light when it was dark outside, which it is a LOT through the long, cold Scottish winters.

During our first winter in the house I complained to the Pink House Husband: 'The thermostat says it's warm, but it still FEELS cold...' Pink House Husband promptly vanished, as he tends to do when he senses a Conversation About Decor on the horizon, but I could work this one out on my own. The problem, I realized, came down to colour, specifically the beigey white walls we'd inherited from the previous owners: while inoffensive during the day, at night they became dingy and depressing.

As something of an interiors magazine obsessive, I knew the wisdom was that painting a dark room dark made it feel cosier. The issue was that this was a bright, light room in the daytime, so how to choose a wall colour that didn't detract from that, while warming up the long dark nights? One trillion sample pots later, I discovered the delights of Manor House Gray: a rich mid-grey from Farrow & Ball. Now when it got dark the room maintained the same warm, friendly feel that it had during the day. It genuinely felt warmer than before we'd painted it, even though we knew it was exactly the same temperature. Here's to darker shades in light rooms – because we should never forget that even the lightest rooms get dark sometimes.

Our family room in London is open plan to the kitchen too, but that's where the rooms' similarities end. Instead of having a large south-facing window, this room is deep within the

**ABOVE RIGHT** Pink flowers are an excellent way to add a rose tint to your home, especially if you have a pink-averse other half, as mine used to be.

**ABOVE** The green velvet IKEA sofa survived two small, messy boys remarkably well; we had it for five years before I sold it on eBay for a decent price.

house; the only natural light comes from the glass door and windows at the kitchen end. And by the time I came to renovate this space, I'd learned lots more interior war-winning skills, meaning much more pink decor. Yay.

I started by painting the space in Farrow & Ball's pale pink Calamine - the same colour I used in my Edinburgh bedroom - but the lack of natural light plus the pink neon sign rendered the paint shade unrecognizable as an actual colour. It just felt dull, pale and – yes – dingy. As did the room itself.

There was only one thing for it: a vibrant peachy pink (Ida by Painthouse), which was applied to the walls during a family holiday. On our return, Pink House Husband had rather a shock (I may have neglected to mention exactly what was happening, colour-wise), but once I'd filled the room with plants, books and feel-good furniture and the neon was emitting its warm glow, everything was just peachy. Now it's the perfect spot to curl up and watch family life unfold/break up fights. Bliss.

**PAGES 86–87** Touches of orange and green visually unite the Edinburgh family room with the open-plan kitchen. The walnut breakfast bar was custom-made by a local furniture maker.

**OPPOSITE** In the absence of cornicing/crown molding, a mid-century-style statement pendant lamp from West Elm adds interest to the upper part of the London family room. The cushions are from House of Hackney, Elizabeth Scarlett and Barbara

Coupe and the rug is a vintage Beni Ourain from Larusi.

**ABOVE RIGHT** We no longer have a cat, but even if we did, there's no way it would dare jump on our Sofas & Stuff corner sofa, which is upholstered in Ian Mankin's Haworth Grey wool.

**RIGHT** This is my favourite lamp – a vintage number sourced from The Old Cinema. It looks lovely next to a Jacqueline Colley print of The Barbican.

**THIS PAGE** This side of the family room combines real plants with a 'living wall' of leafy art. I'm a big fan of macramé plant holders; they're perfect for displaying pretty trailing plants, which tumble down to fill awkward spaces.

## SIX NON-PLASTICKY STORAGE IDEAS FOR TOYS

**1 VINTAGE SIDEBOARDS** The drawers are great for pens, paper and small toys, while the cupboards hold board games.

**2 SUITCASES** I have peachy pink metal ones that are perfect for small-piece construction toys like Lego, plus they slide under my sideboard.

**3 ALPHABET DRAWERS** The alphabet chest in my Edinburgh family room had a playful feel, and the shallow drawers made it easy to find small items.

**4 LARGE FABRIC BASKETS** Great for those mountains of soft toys and the more unwieldy toys that you always trip over in the middle of the night.

**5 UNDER–SOFA STORAGE** Pink House Husband made extra-shallow 'drawers' from cut-down cardboard boxes so thatthey slid out of sight under our green velvet sofa.

**6 THE WASTE BASKET** This is a hugely underestimated storage solution that clears broken toys in no time (TIP: make that sure no children are watching during this particular clear-up session).

**ABOVE LEFT** I couldn't resist this pink marble shelf with gold brackets from Graham & Green. A string of hearts plant and a few beautiful books finish off this corner nicely.

**ABOVE** This bird lamp base used to be silver, but in a rare DIY moment I spray-painted it gold to match the handmade marbled lampshade from Munro and Kerr.

**OPPOSITE** The view from the family room through the dining area out to the sunny, south-facing garden makes this one of my favourite spots to sit in the house.

# Pinkspiration

Anna Atwal is the founder of fabulous interiors store Pad Lifestyle (@padlifestyle), and this swoon-worthy space is the family room she designed for her Edinburgh home, where she lives with husband Haj and seven-year-old son Leo.

**Q** Did you plan for this room to pay homage to pink?

**A** It wasn't my intention to create a pink room, but I really wanted that specific pink sofa...

**Q** What was the starting point for the design?

**A** First I painted the whole room white, including the floorboards. It's the most beautiful room in the house with the best light and best views, so stripping it right back to start with allowed me to work with the space and the layout.

**Q** What kind of a vibe were you after in here?

**A** I wanted to combine modern touches and period details to create a comfortable yet glamorous space, using our favourite art, objects and furniture to add colour and personality.

**Q** Did your husband have any input?

**A** My husband's taste is here too with all the art we have collected, and he loves the burled mappa wood Bond range by Jonathan Adler. He didn't know the giant pink sofa was coming, but he loves that now too, even though it's not something he'd have thought to choose himself.

**Q** As the only girl in the house, do you think it's especially important to decorate with pink?

**A** If you love pink, then why not use that colour? I don't think it has anything to do with gender – for me, pink simply says 'happy'! My husband loves this room too.

**Q** Can a glamorous home be a practical family home?

**A** Of course! You can have a practical room layout, but still be glamorous with your style and with colour. My room designs for our family home start with personality, lifestyle and what I love.

**Q** When it comes to finding the perfect family sofa, what do you look for?

**A** A family sofa needs to be comfy and big enough for everyone to lounge on it. This sofa is also great, as it keeps its shape so you don't have to keep fluffing it up after sitting on it.

**Q** How did you include the TV in the room's design?

**A** I didn't attempt to hide it, as it is pretty huge – my husband likes a big TV – but I hung our biggest artworks either side as a distraction. I also deliberately created two seating zones in the room, with the TV and sofa on one side and then the cosy wing chairs by the traditional fireplace on the other.

**Q** What colour goes best with pink?

**A** Green for sure. A match made in heaven!

# 6

# The Bedroom

I planned my Edinburgh bedroom around a pink velvet armchair that I bought way back when the Pink House Husband was still the Rented Flat Boyfriend. You may be surprised to learn that this little chair is one of Pink House Husband's favourites – until you discover that's because 'when I sit on it, I don't have to look at it' (eyes-to-the-sky emoji).

The chair informed the iridescent purple wallpaper with its hot pink butterflies (and nasty-looking insects; the subversion appealed to Pink House Husband), the green velvet curtains (because pink and green is always a good idea) and the grey wool carpet (ditto).

However, this room is the perfect example of what happens if you don't finish the decorating job completely. Much as I loved the elements just mentioned, I didn't love the bed or bedside tables/nightstands – they were a never-been-replaced relic from the days when I thought shabby chic was a good idea. Just for the record: shabby chic is NEVER a good idea.

In my new London home, I was determined that things would be different. This time I WOULD decorate from start to finish, and I wouldn't live with anything I didn't love.

**RIGHT** I loved the Timorous Beasties wallpaper and pale pink walls in my Edinburgh bedroom – they're Farrow & Ball's Calamine – but I wish I'd replaced the bed with a padded yellow or pink velvet headboard.

**THIS PAGE** White neon lightening bolts from bag&bones add an urban touch to this room with its views of London, and tie in with the white zig-zag cushions from Projektityyny.

This approach didn't get off to a promising start. I'd no sooner ordered samples of my favourite pink wallpaper (Rabarber by Gocken Jobs) when the Pink House Husband put his foot down. Apparently I was not allowed to use either a) pattern on the walls or b) pink on the walls. I was informed that this was 'my bedroom too' and that he'd 'had enough pink' and patterned wallpaper was 'clutter'. For all my war-winning ways, even I can admit when I'm beaten. But this wasn't one of those times.

With Pink House Husband's strict wall-related prohibitions, it fell to the floor to pick up the pink-patterned gauntlet. I'd had my eye on this Liberty shell print carpet for a while – finally, I had the perfect opportunity to use it! Pattern on the floor and on the walls might have been too much, but as the walls had to stay plain, I could go for it underfoot. And much as I love a reclaimed wooden floorboard, there's absolutely nothing like a dense wool carpet to welcome your toes on a cold winter's morning.

The bed (made to my own specification by Hypnos) was another triumph of pink – strictly speaking, a headboard isn't a wall, but it still allowed me to add my favourite hue to a vertical surface.

I agonized over the wall colour. At first I was going to go grey. But then I thought, 'Do I really want to wake to grey every day? Wouldn't blue be better?' And it is.

**ABOVE LEFT** This is a ceramic cheetah lampstand from House of Hackney – the pair of lamps were a birthday present to myself from myself.

**ABOVE CENTRE** Pattern on pattern is easier to get right than you might think, especially when starting with this coral pink Capello Shell carpet from Alternative Flooring.

**ABOVE RIGHT** I designed the Hypnos headboard, right down to the slope of the curves and spacing of the brass studs.

Although it's a weird quirk of this particular shade of blue (Farrow & Ball's Oval Room Blue) that 50% of people who walk into my bedroom think it's green.

And then the finishing touches: ceramic cheetah lamps, fringed shades, neon bolts and a dreamy swimming pool print and you have a bedroom that makes me want to dive right in. Pink House Husband is happy too. Phew!

**LEFT** This hydrangea from Hayford & Rhodes is just the perfect shade of sugary pink. It makes me smile first thing in the morning.

**CENTRE LEFT** Details matter. The shell-like knobs on my Graham & Green chest of drawers match the shell pattern in the carpet. Sigh.

**BOTTOM LEFT** More knobs, this time knurled brass beauties from Buster + Punch on my wardrobe. I like to contrast pretty decor with a bit of utilitarian rock chic.

**OPPOSITE** I used to think colour coding books disrespected their contents. Now I realize that is utter rubbish. Bring on the pretty literary rainbow!

## FIVE STORAGE SOLUTIONS FOR SMALL BEDROOMS

1 **BUILT-IN FLOOR-TO-CEILING STORAGE** Paint it the same colour as the walls so that it doesn't overpower the space.

2 **CHESTS OF DRAWERS AS BEDSIDE TABLES/ NIGHTSTANDS** Check the height before buying; they should be convenient for your coffee cup.

3 **UNDER-BED STORAGE** Our kingsize bed holds 54 pairs of shoes. Pink House Husband keeps his in the wardrobe/closet.

4 **AN OTTOMAN** Mine is not only a vision of beauty in House of Hackney velvet, but stores all my gym kit while providing a place to sit.

5 **USE THE LANDING** There's no space in our bedroom for my dressing table, so I've moved it to just outside the door, using space that would otherwise have been wasted.

# Pinkspiration

Artist Residence (@artistresidence) describes itself as 'an eccentric bunch of fun and friendly boutique hotels', and having stayed in many of their luxe-yet-homely rooms, I wholeheartedly agree. I chatted to Justin Salisbury, who co-owns Artist Residence with wife Charlie, to find out what makes the perfect bedroom.

**Q** When it comes to designing one of your hotel bedrooms, where do you start?

**A** The most important thing is comfort, so finding great beds is key. We often custom-build our beds to get exactly what we want. Another crucial area that's often neglected is lighting and power. I love dimmer switches – they're so much better in bedrooms than overhead lights that are super-bright all the time. When it comes to bedside sockets, they should be positioned just behind the bedside table/nightstand. If you're renovating, always put in more sockets than you think you'll need.

**Q** Do you and Charlie agree on interior design decisions?

**A** We used to do everything together – serving breakfast, designing the rooms – but as the company has grown, our roles have had to change. Charlie's the one with business skills, so she runs the company now – she's happy to hand the interiors side over to me. She's a great sounding board when it comes to discussing designs though.

**Q** I love how each Artist Residence room has a distinct personality, but is there a common design thread?

**A** We work with nice old buildings with lots of character. Our job is mainly un-decorating – opening up ceilings to reveal old beams, beautiful brickwork and architectural features. I want to create spaces that look like they've always been like that – my biggest fear is to over-design. Then we bring in reclaimed and vintage furniture – it gets better with age and is practical for withstanding wear and tear. We take a similar approach to our family home.

**Q** What's your attitude to colour when designing a room?

**A** We tend to stick to a muted palette to keep things as timeless as possible, then use colour in artworks and accessories to juxtapose the original features and add a splash of modernity. Pink looks great in vintage Moroccan rugs especially. And we love pink neon! But on the whole, we've learned that bold schemes don't lend themselves well to a good night's sleep; a bedroom should feel relaxed.

**Q** What's your favourite Artist Residence bedroom and why?

**A** The grand suite in London is pretty good [talk about an understatement – it's bloody gorgeous! EM]. Large rooms are really hard – there are many more options. We weren't so confident in our design abilities back when we renovated that room, but we made up for our lack of experience by spending lots of time on the building site. The builders hated me – I kept changing my mind over and over!

# 7

# The Bathroom

Once upon a time, I loved to laze in gorgeous boutique hotels –
in their bathrooms in particular. I would wallow in freestanding
tubs; warm, scented bubbles popping around me, a glass of cold
bubbles in my hand, with absolutely no one pestering me to swap
the blue beaker for the red one, or chastising me for not cutting
the cake into two perfectly equal parts. When I gained a baby,
I lost my boutique bathtub days. Because of my dramatic reaction
to this tragic loss, the Pink House Husband agreed that I could
convert the tiny family bathroom in our Edinburgh house into
the world's smallest spa. Only one catch: it couldn't be pink.

One thing you'll notice about boutique spa bathrooms: they don't have loads of crap lying about (literally and metaphorically). So my first job was to make best use of every inch of space in the bathroom to store stuff away. This I did by having my builders create an under-sink cabinet for all the kiddie clutter, and recessed, tiled shelves behind the bathtub and above the loo (inspired by my boutique hotel fave, Babington House) for easy-access items. In the over-toilet recess, I curated a little selection of books to create a 'loobrary' (I TOTALLY invented this word). The prettiest products were displayed on down-lit glass shelves in the top section of a bespoke cabinet behind the door, with not-so-pretty products hidden away behind doors in the bottom section.

One of our tiny bathroom's main problems was the lack of shower - the ceiling slopes, so there's not enough space to stand in the bathtub. Yes, we had a shower room, but that was two flights down from my bedroom, and I didn't love being surprised by the supermarket delivery man in nothing but a towel.

But who says you have to stand up in the shower? Instead, I had a lovely brass sit-down shower installed. And you know what? It's excellent for shaving your legs (sitting = easy leg access). Post sit-down shower, I rarely encountered random men while half-naked in my hallway, though some might argue that this isn't necessarily a benefit.

With all the practical problems overcome, it was time to get decorating. Lashings of brass and dark grey paint (Downpipe by Farrow & Ball) for starters, with a marble sink surround for glamour. But without pink permission, I needed to get creative for that wow-factor boutique hit. Wallpaper was the obvious answer. With the rest of the room decked out in white, grey and gold, pretty any design and colour combo was an option. Approximately 23 million wallpaper samples later and I'd chosen...the first sample I'd looked at. As a colour lover I'd expected to choose a full-on multi-coloured design, but these serene gold koi carp circling around a sedate pond just whispered 'spa' to me. A little pink pot of flowers (ha!) and my beautiful spa bathroom was complete.

## HOW TO TURN YOUR BATHROOM INTO A SPA

**SCENTED CANDLE** Buy the best one you can afford – and yes, how it looks is just as important as how it smells

**TEA LIGHTS** Because one candle is never enough – scatter tea lights on every available (safe) surface, then turn off the electric lights.

**CLEAN FLUFFY BATHMAT** Don't ruin the blissful experience by lowering your feet onto a damp, flat, manky mat.

**MUSIC** If you don't have built-in bathroom speakers (a worthwhile investment), your phone will do – the tunes are up to you, but I'd advise against thrash metal.

**POSH EXFOLIATOR** For that just-been-scrubbed spa sensation; I love Trish McEvoy's Blackberry & Vanilla Sugar Scrub.

**BOOZE** Pink champagne FTW.

**OPPOSITE BOTTOM**
Brass taps/faucets were one of my bathroom must-haves. I love how they age naturally, giving them a vintage patina that contrasts with the bright, white tiles.

**FAR RIGHT** Wallpaper* City Guides are my favourite travel guides – and the rainbow covers look lovely in a 'loobrary'.

**RIGHT** Been given a pink decor prohibition by your other half? Just say the shade with flowers instead!

# Pinkspiration

This bathroom is the master en suite in a beautiful 19th-century seven-bedroom country house in Oxfordshire. It was designed by the house's owner, mum-of-four Kate Jones. Kate spends her weekends here with husband Henry and the kids (aged between six and twelve). During the week the family live in their London apartment.

**Q** Is this your favourite room in the house?

**A** Yes it is – not just because of how the room looks, but how I spend my time here. If I'm in this bathroom, it's the weekend and I'm getting ready in an unhurried way. Sometimes the kids will join me – we'll turn the music up and have a 'disco bath' where we all rock out!

**Q** What inspired the colour of this room?

**A** For me, picking wall colours is all about how light plays into the room. This bathroom and the bedroom it opens onto has windows on three sides, so is incredibly bright. I thought this would suit a warm, feminine shade on the walls; this is Pink Ground by Farrow & Ball and it reminds me of the blush warmth of my favourite Provence rosé wine. Plus this colour works so well with the marble and brass.

**Q** What does your husband think of his pink bathroom?

**A** Honestly? He's never even commented on it! He doesn't get involved in any design decisions; I didn't tell him my decorating plans for this room – or any of the rooms in this house. He's used to it now, and he always like the rooms when they're finished. In fact, no one has ever commented on the pinkness of this room – it's not an in-your-face colour, but incredibly calming.

**Q** So you don't think men feel threatened by pink?

**A** Not my husband anyway - he even has a pink suit! One of the guest bedrooms in this house is painted a brighter pink – Nancy's Blushes by Farrow & Ball. Loads of men stay there and they don't make a fuss. Though my brother, who is a regular guest, does call it the Liberace suite...

**Q** What do you like most about the room?

**A** I love the seating section in the middle, between the bathroom and bedroom. I can sit here after my bath and flick through a magazine. Or someone else can sit here and chat to me while I'm in the tub. And the hotel vibes of the double sink unit really do it for me too. I had it made to look like a unit in my favourite hotel – Ett Hem in Stockholm.

# 8

# The Kids' Rooms

Why is there no pink in my kids' rooms? It's a very good question, and I'm not sure I have a definitive answer. The most obvious response is because I have two boys. But, of course, that would fly in the face of my belief that pink is a colour for people, not just little girls. Isn't it amazing, though, how much we're influenced by societal norms, even when we're determined not to be?

The second potential answer is because I wanted a girl. Important note: Don't get me wrong; I couldn't love my incredible, gorgeous, funny, clever, caring boys any more than I do, but I always wanted to experience the mother-daughter relationship from the other side, partly because I have a great relationship with my own mum, and partly because girls are AWESOME.

I'm very open about this now, but when I decorated these rooms in my Edinburgh house a few years ago, I hadn't quite made peace with the fact that I'd never have a daughter (three kids is not for me). But why would wanting a girl and not admitting it mean no pink in the boys' rooms? The massively flawed logic goes that I didn't want people to think I was trying to wish my beautiful boys into girls by using a 'feminine' colour to decorate their rooms. Crazy. But true.

The third and final part-answer is that my eldest, Oscar, had already shown himself to be a huge fan of all things pirate, rocket and wheeled vehicle. And the sad fact was that these things are hard to come by in pink. Had I been looking for them in that shade. Which I wasn't - see part-answers one and two above.

**ABOVE LEFT** Chalkboard paint on the cupboard doors gave Oscar (and me!) a space to express himself in his loft bedroom without drawing on the actual walls (though he did that too...).

**LEFT** I chose this Ferm Living wallpaper for my younger son Zac's room because it was fun, stylish and gender neutral.

**THIS PAGE** I kept things simple in Zac's room, as I knew we'd be moving house fairly soon. The walls are Teresa's Green from Farrow & Ball and I picked up the little green stool from a local vintage shop.

**OPPOSITE** My sleep-deprived self fell for these square wooden Ferm Living pictures, as they had a nostalgic quality that reminded me of my own childhood.

**RIGHT** I sourced this dark blue Pirate Seas illustrated wallpaper from Hibou Home for treasure-hunter Oscar, and paired it with walls painted in Farrow & Ball's blue/grey Lamp Room Gray. Similar hand-knitted personalized bunting can be found on Etsy.

## MY FAVOURITE THINGS ABOUT THESE ROOMS

**1** The Z A C knobs I added to the blue IKEA chest of drawers.

**2** The Ferm Living green animal wallpaper - Scandi brands often have a great gender-neutral selection of kids decor.

**3** Blackboard paint on the lower cupboards made the most of limited vertical space in Oscar's attic bedroom.

**4** The Oliver Bonas teal velvet tub chair - the perfect size for mum-and-son stories.

**5** The flattened badger rug - in the depths of sleep deprivation, it made me smile.

The reality of the decor in these rooms is that they were designed by a mum - me! - who hadn't come to terms with her new maternal role. Yes, they were bright and colourful and based on things the boys enjoyed, but the honest truth was I didn't want to be in them. I wanted to be on my own, reading a book in the sitting room. Or drinking cocktails at Soho House in a dress that no longer fitted me and I no longer owned.

We're about to start renovating the kids' rooms in our London home, and I feel completely differently this time - about the rooms, and about who I am. My boys are no longer boys - well they are, but first and foremost they're PEOPLE. People I love spending time with. People who no longer need their nappies changed. People who can carefully articulate their thoughts, feelings and preferences, and play The Game of Life with me (both literally and metaphorically) without anyone bursting into tears.

So will the boys' new bedrooms include pink? I do have a definitive answer to this question: I really don't care, so long as a) they love them, and b) I love them. Because I'm looking forward to spending some quality time in there. I've come a long way, and I'm not just talking about the 500 miles from Scotland.

# Pinkspiration

This perfectly pink room belongs to five-year-old Grace Nickolls, who lives in a four-bedroom detached 1980s house in Buckinghamshire with baby brother Jake, dad Trev and mum Vickie, an interior decorator (@interior.therapy). I chatted to Vickie about how she designed the space and her tips for stylish kids' rooms.

**Q** How did you expect Grace's room to be used?

**A** I wanted to create a room for sleeping and playing, so I added enough storage so she could keep most of her toys in her room. With a new baby brother we wanted her to have a space of her own where she could play with friends.

**Q** Do you see the room's usage changing as Grace gets older?

**A** I added a desk for this reason, as I want this room to be her quiet space to do homework over the coming years. It's also why I've gone for a look that's girlie and not too grown up, but can be easily updated with new prints or accessories when her tastes change.

**Q** How did you choose the paint colour?

**A** Grace asked if she could have pink walls in her bedroom - it's her favourite colour, so how could I refuse? I also love pink, but find it hard to get it past the husband, so we mainly have pink accessories instead of walls in our house.

**Q** Why did you only paint the pink up part of the wall?

**A** I had seen half-painted rooms and loved the concept, but hadn't found the perfect room for it yet. Once I'd chosen the paint colour - Benjamin Moore's Rosetone - I decided it was a little strong to use across every wall, so the half-wall effect was perfect.

**Q** How did you decide where to paint?

**A** I painted the pink less than halfway up the wall, allowing the expanse of white above to create a bright, airy effect - great for a room like this with a fairly low ceiling. This also gave me more space to hang prints above the line.

**Q** Any tips on choosing and hanging art in a child's room?

**A** Most of the prints and artwork in my house are from independent sellers on Instagram; there's so much choice and it's fun discovering new artists. I like to hang larger prints on their own, but also love creating little gallery walls of prints I've collected, to give more impact (see p.57 for tips on creating the perfect gallery wall).

**Q** How does Grace like her new room?

**A** She just loves it! She especially adores having all her toys in her bedroom. She's a big fan of her new desk too, and has already started to use it for drawing.

# 9

# The Home Office

I didn't have a home office in my Edinburgh house. At the time at least one of my kids was at the age where as soon as you merely think about sitting down to do some work that doesn't involve being a little teapot, both short and stout (I blame the chocolate Hobnobs for the stout part), the cry will go up: 'Mummyyyyy! I need a wee weeeee!' And so a home office wasn't really required.

But kids grow up, and I am not one to be sentimental about this fact. Indeed, while dropping the youngest off for his first day of school, weeping parents hand-wringing around the playground, me and my equally callous Pink House Husband shared a high five and headed off for a boozy brunch.

Now my kids are both at school, I have some time to get shit done again – hence this book! And my London home office.

**RIGHT** It doesn't get much better than these pink Pradena encaustic tiles from Bert & May. I'd like to tile my entire London hallway in them.

**BELOW LEFT** This is the Mathieu Challières La Volière table lamp, which used to live in my Edinburgh dining room. It's one of my more controversial pieces of decor – people tend to love it or hate it. Guess which camp my husband falls into?

**OPPOSITE** Bespoke shelves contain books, magazines, styling props, prized possessions and pink gin. On the wall is a limited-edition pink-and-gold Grayson Perry 'Kateboard' depicting the Duchess of Cambridge.

Isn't it funny how once you're allowed the thing you really want, you don't want it any more? I've spent the past seven years trying to coerce Pink House Husband into allowing me to paint things pink, and now, faced with a room of my own that I can colour any hue I choose, I've gone for grey.

But there's method in my madness: as I explained in The Exterior chapter (see p.18), dark grey and pink is a winning combo for me. And, as I'm learning, you don't need to reinvent the colour wheel in every single room. So the thought process behind the grey walls was partly that it would prove the perfect foil for pink in its various shades. Plus, this rich, dark grey (Farrow & Ball's Downpipe) has a cocooning effect I find conducive to calm concentration in a way that, say, four walls of full-on fuchsia might not be.

Design-wise, the room centres on the original fireplace. Hearths have always held a special place in my heart, and pretty little corner

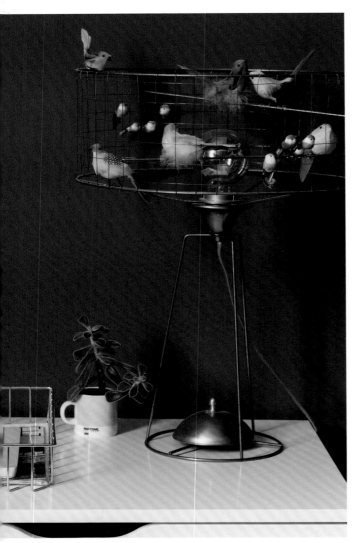

**OPPOSITE** As this is a small room, I didn't want the furniture to feel overwhelming. A smoked glass desk from Made.com and a Perspex Kartell Ghost chair blend into the background, and I added a blush pink velvet House Doctor cushion for extra comfort - and extra pink. The gold basket is from Paperchase.

**ABOVE** The London Curtain Girls made this Roman blind for me using Emma J Shipley cotton satin Audubon fabric, and the Samuel & Sons Dolce pompom fringe in Sugarplum.

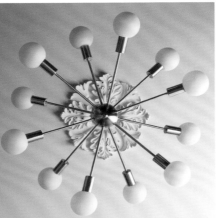

hearths with the original fire surround are particularly special. But I didn't like the bare metal, so asked my decorator to paint it white, aside from the innermost section. Now the fireplace pops against the walls.

The starting point for the pinkification of this room was the ceiling, for which I chose the most delicate of pinks (Middleton Pink by Farrow & Ball). This is a shade I've wanted to use for ages, but lacked the necessary Pink House Husband approval. Now when I look heavenward in search of inspiration there it is: the pink of dreams. Like the prettiest of pictures, the ceiling deserved the perfect frame, so I had cornicing/crown molding installed that referenced the Edwardian era of the house

– nothing too fussy, though, as this is a small room. And to draw the eye up, a fabulous Sputnik-style lamp, surrounded by a bespoke ceiling rose that Cornice London meticulously installed, piece by delicate plaster piece.

Other must-have items include the pink encaustic cement star tiles in the hearth that Pink House Husband refused to allow in the kitchen, and a pink-and-gold rug I used in a photoshoot and fell in love with. Finally, the Kama Sutra print with pink sparkly letters found its natural home over the mantelpiece. This print reminds me of my days editing the sex pages of *more!* magazine, bending fake Barbies and Kens into eye-watering positions. It's good to be reminded of past masterpieces.

# *Quiz* WHICH PINK BEST REFLECTS YOUR PERSONALITY?

Pink comes in many shades, so when you're making decor decisions it's useful to know which pink clan you belong to. Try this quiz on your partner as well – once they realize there's a pink crew for them too, the interior war is halfway won.

### 1 WHAT'S YOUR IDEAL WAY TO SPEND A SATURDAY NIGHT?

A) Sipping champagne at the opera
B) With a couple of cans of spray paint – and no one watching
C) Stargazing in a field
D) Dancing on a podium

### 2 WHICH OF THESE FAMOUS PEOPLE WOULD YOU PREFER AS A GUEST AT YOUR DINNER PARTY?

A) Audrey Hepburn
B) Pablo Escobar
C) David Attenborough
D) Courtney Love

### 3 WHAT'S YOUR BEST CHILD-WRANGLING TECHNIQUE?

A) Speaking as softly as possible so that they have to be quiet to hear you
B) Let them watch a movie: *The Great Escape* is educational
C) Head outside – nature is the best babysitter
D) Make placards and take them on a demonstration

### 4 MIX ME A DRINK – WHAT'S YOUR COCKTAIL OF CHOICE?

A) Vodka Martini – but not because of James Bond
B) French 75 – it was invented during Prohibition you know
C) Hibiscus Margaritas – served in the garden
D) Porn-star Martini

### 5 WHAT'S YOUR DREAM HOLIDAY DESTINATION?

A) The Amalfi Coast
B) Anywhere with sheltered coves
C) Madagascar
D) Rio de Janeiro

### 6 WHICH SONG BEST SUMS YOU UP?

A) Carmen by Georges Bizet
B) Smooth Criminal by Michael Jackson
C) English Country Garden by Jimmie Rodgers
D) Get the Party Started by Pink

### 7 WHO IS YOUR FASHION ICON?

A) Christian Dior – *naturellement!*
B) Paul Smith – he's all about the stripes
C) Stella McCartney – no animals are harmed in the making of her clothes
D) Vivienne Westwood – her designs make a real impact

### 8 WHICH VEHICLE ARE YOU MOST DRAWN TO?

A) A vintage Rolls Royce
B) A police car
C) A bicycle
D) A brand new Tesla

**MOSTLY As:** PARED-BACK BLUSH
You're a sophisticated sort – proof that pink lovers can be as cool as they come. Turn to p.102–3 and p.28–9 for rooms I've decorated using pink as a neutral, and p.21 for my interview with dusky pink lover Victoria Metaxas.

**MOSTLY Bs:** BAKER-MILLER PINK
We're not saying you have felonious tendencies, but you're definitely drawn to a shade of pink that studies have shown to have a calming effect on criminals. See p.31 for a chat with Charlie Mills about why his team painted a car park staircase in Baker-Miller Pink and called it art

**MOSTLY Cs:** FRESHEST FUCHSIA/RAMBLING ROSE
Yes, you care about your home, but if you're honest you'd rather be outside and your love of a plant-related pink reflects that. For tips on how to bring the outdoors into your home, see p.37.

**MOSTLY Ds:** KICK-ASS NEON
Whatever you do, you do it loud and proud. You love a slogan tee as much as an air guitar solo. For tips on decorating with hot pink, see overleaf for my interview with Gigi Foyle from bag&bones.

# Pinkspiration

Gigi Foyle is the co-founder of bag&bones (@bagandbones), an environmentally sustainable, kid-proof LED neon brand selling its own designs, as well as offering a bespoke service. Besides having a cool home office of her own, Gigi has installed neon in some of the UK's most creative workspaces.

**Q** What are the most important things to consider when designing the perfect office?

**A** I've always been interested in the psychology of colour. Whenever we're working with a client, the first thing I ask is what kind of mood do you want to achieve? Then I'll suggest a colour to match. Plus, if you're anything like me, then your mind works better when there's less clutter – keeping everything quite minimal helps with this. Although by the end of the day my desk is piled high with lights, paperwork and an ever-growing to-do list...

**Q** What's the coolest office you've ever been into?

**A** The Kate Moss Agency was pretty cool. I was expecting something quite flash, but it was understated and minimal – white walls, white sofa, white flowers. Obviously they went for a white bag&bones neon.

**Q** How do you recommend adding neon to an office without it being distracting?

**A** I often recommend blues, whites and paler colours to create a calm, less-distracting ambience. But sometimes our creative clients want to give their office a party, high-energy vibe and we've installed lots of hot pink neon lights in offices across London!

**Q** What inspires your neon designs?

**A** Living and working in London inspires me. There's beautiful street art and graffiti around every corner, and some of the best museums in the world. I will never run out of ideas so long as I'm roaming the streets of London. We're also heavily influenced by music. The radio is on pretty much all day at bag&bones HQ, and a certain tune or song lyric will spark a new idea and we'll start doodling away.

**Q** If someone was thinking about commissioning a bespoke neon sign, what advice would you give them?

**A** Keep the designs to basic line drawings. Neon works best when it's simple – aesthetically and in terms of affordability. If you're searching for a symbol or slogan that means something special, tattoos and song lyrics are a good place to start.

**Q** What's the best bespoke sign you've ever made?

**A** We re-created that iconic neon from *Batman Returns*: the sign flashes between 'HELLO THERE' and 'HELL HERE'. For a Catwoman fan, it's pretty hard to top that.

**Q** Why is pink neon so damn fine?

**A** There is just something about hot pink neon that get's people going. It gives off the most amazing glow – vibrant and sexy. I just can't get enough of it!

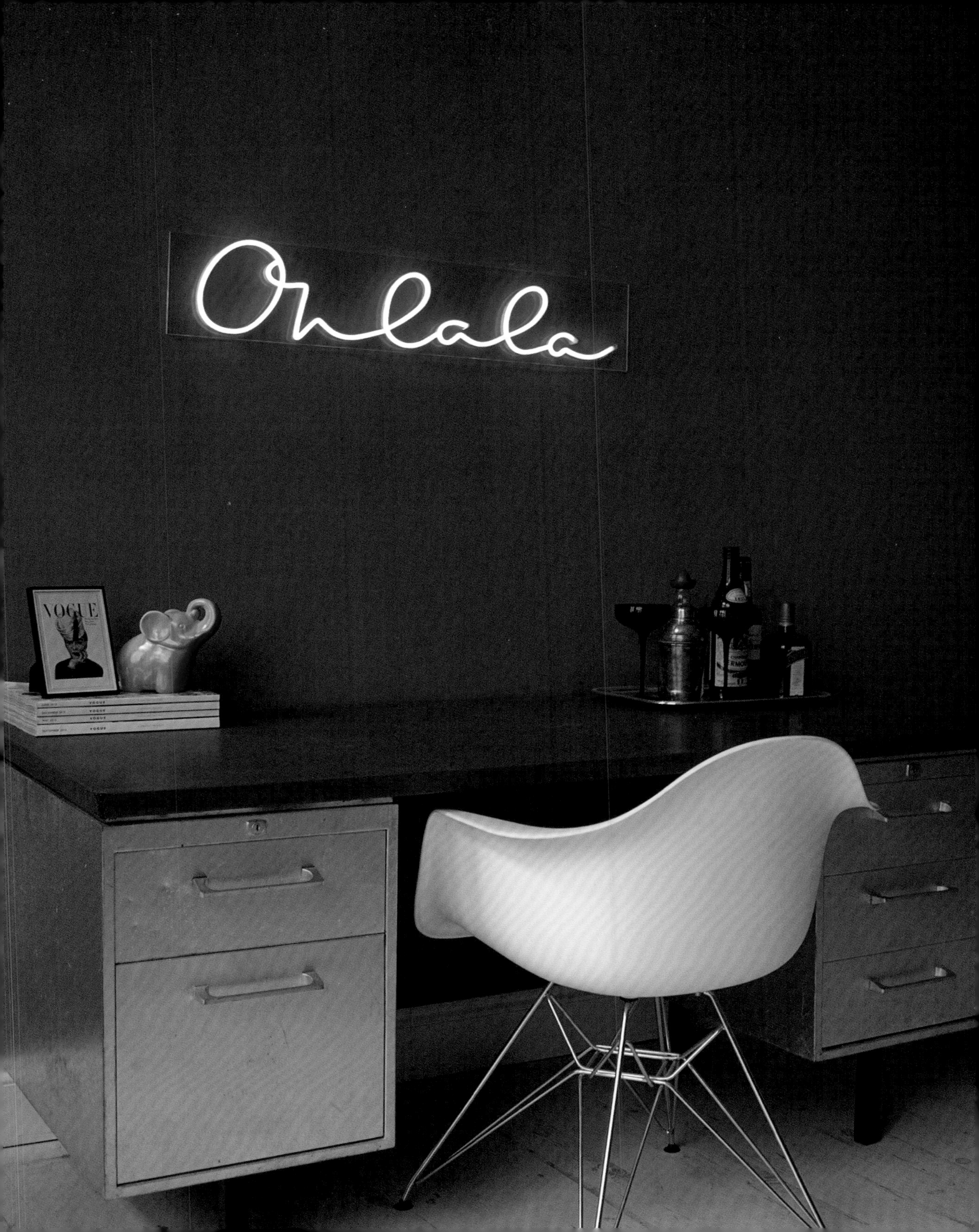
VOGUE

# 10

# The Garden

The house where I grew up had a wonderful garden, with a large daisy-strewn lawn, veg patch and pretty herbaceous borders. My mum was the green-fingered head gardener who grew pink potatoes, sweet green peas-in-the-pod and juicy courgettes/zucchini with vibrant yellow flowers. She also had an eye for garden design, an understanding of which shrubs grew well where and a dedication to deadheading and careful pruning.

I loved the garden, and as a young girl would sit among the speedwells, threading daisy chains and checking for any signs of fairies. The apple tree at the bottom of the garden was my special spot, where I would sit reading a book. The tang of the flowering redcurrant; the heavy scent of the lilac; the roses' heady perfume – this was what my childhood smelled like.

But much in the same way that childhood camping holidays have resulted in an adult obsession with posh hotels, my early years grubbing in the potato patch have rendered me reluctant to get my hands dirty in my own garden. Instead, I appreciate the gardens of others (along with her herbaceous borders, my mother now has an authentic alpine rockery, a preponderance of blue poppies and a stone trough of succulents). But when it comes to my own home, I go for fresh flowers IN the house, and carefully styled - and very clean - decor outside.

While the house's interior is my domain, the garden is very much the property of the Pink House Husband. A farmer's son, he relishes the horticultural challenge of whipping nature into shape, and has been steadily taming our London garden since we arrived, despite the kids' best efforts to ruin the lawn and destroy entire trees with their soccer.

However, my version of gardening focuses on creating cute spaces to eat, drink and lounge around. With this in mind, I've created three distinct areas in my 'outdoor room' (see left).

## MY GARDEN ZONES

**THE COCKTAIL JUNGLE** This is a comfy outdoor sofa for two on the patio surrounded by tropical plants (in pots – no need for actual planting). A string of outdoor lights means there's no need to give up on the Aperol Spritz alfresco just because the sun's gone down. Once the lemons on my tiny citrus trees have ripened, there'll be no need for Pink House Husband to go in to fetch the garnish either. Now I just need an outdoor fridge...

**THE LUNCHEON NOOK** Perfect for when the girls come round on a sunny Saturday. The kids get locked inside with *The Lion King* and we lunch off this white marble table in a ladylike fashion while using unladylike language to describe our offspring's latest exploits.

**THE BREAKFAST BAY** Tucked alongside the pond, this is where I like to escape solo in the morning because ideally another human being shouldn't utter a word to me until I've had my eyes open for at least 45 minutes and have drunk approximately 3.5 coffees. Hence my sweary mug, which says 'I'm not a morning person, so kindly...' on the other side.

#  Pinkspiration

I've been obsessed with fellow pink lovers Graham & Green since I walked
into their treasure trove of a Primrose Hill boutique more than 10 years ago.
Here I grill Lou Graham, who runs the family business with husband Jamie,
on patios, plants and (of course) pink.

**Q** What are your tips for styling a garden space?

**A** Treat your garden just like any other room in your home: start with the essentials – furniture and lighting – then layer on textiles and accessories that can easily be moved inside. Like your home, your outdoor space should be filled with things that make you smile, and colour is the perfect way to achieve this.

**Q** Which plants would you suggest work well in pots on the patio or windowsill?

**A** Leafy ferns are brilliant for the windowsill, they are low maintenance and instantly refresh a space. Our patio is filled with plants that help the bees: lavender, alliums and wild flowers.

**Q** What are your signature eat-outside dishes?

**A** When the sun is shining, the last thing on your mind is a hot meal, so our go-to alfresco favourite is grilled goat's cheese drizzled with honey, lots of fig jam and a fresh tomato salad with plenty of seasoning.

**Q** You feature plenty of pink in your home and garden decor – why is this?

**A** From subtle blush tones that soften contemporary spaces, to rich, vibrant pinks that instantly draw the eye; there's a space for pink in almost any setting! Gardens are often quite a blank canvas, so you can afford to be bold with bright pink without it being too much.

**Q** Is pink decor more popular now than it has been?

**A** Definitely. Interior trends over the past few years have demonstrated how versatile the colour can be, and people are being braver about moving away from boring beige and adding colour to their homes.

**Q** Blush pink or hot pink and why?

**A** Definitely hot pink, specifically the rani pink of the Rajputi turban that you see in Jaipur, India. It is the very essence of the Pink City.

**Q** What colour goes best with pink and why?

**A** Deep orange marigold flowers sit beautifully next to a rich, hot Indian pink.

**Q** What is your favourite pink decor item in your own home?

**A** Without a doubt, it's our feathered flamingo!

# Sources

**ALTERNATIVE FLOORING**
www.alternativeflooring.com
*Patterned and natural fibre carpets, runners and rugs.*

**AMARA LIVING**
www.amara.com
*An online-only collection of designer homeware.*

**ANTHROPOLOGIE**
www.anthropologie.com
*A global collection of homeware, furniture and fashion.*

**BAG & BONES**
www.bagandbones.co.uk
*LED neon lighting and art for sale and hire.*

**BEND GOODS**
www.bendgoods.com
*Powder-coated metal chairs, stool and tables from LA.*

**BERT & MAY**
www.bertandmay.com
*Handmade and reclaimed encaustic tiles, plus bathroom and kitchen fixtures and fittings.*

**BLUEBELLGRAY**
www.bluebellgray.com
*Floral, geometric and abstract patterned textiles and homeware from hand-painted designs.*

**BUSTER + PUNCH**
www.busterandpunch.com
*Lighting, brassware and furniture with an urban vibe.*

**CHRISTOPHER FARR**
www.christopherfarrcloth.com
*London-based textile design studio working with contemporary artists and designers.*

**COLE & SON**
www.cole-and-son.com
*Purveyors of wow-factor printed wallpapers since 1875.*

**DESIGNERS GUILD**
www.designersguild.com
*Fabrics, wallpaper, upholstery, homeware and accessories.*

**ELIZABETH SCARLETT**
www.elizabethscarlett.com
*Embroidered travel-inspired cushions, bedding and travel pouches.*

**EMMA J SHIPLEY**
www.emmajshipley.com
*Graphic artist Emma's intricate pencil drawings turned into home and fashion accessories.*

**FARROW & BALL**
www.farrow-ball.com
*Historically-inspired paint and wallpaper.*

**FERM LIVING**
www.fermliving.com
*Whimsical Danish home accessories with a graphic edge.*

**FOREST LONDON**
www.forest.london
*Plants and products that bring nature into your home.*

**FRANCESCA GENTILLI**
www.francescagentilli.com
*Vintage and bespoke rugs handmade by artisans in India, Morocco and Peru.*

**GRAHAM & GREEN**
www.grahamandgreen.co.uk
*An eclectic range of furniture and home decor sourced from around the world.*

**HAYFORD & RHODES**
www.hayfordandrhodes.co.uk
*Top London florist offering wedding, event and corporate flowers.*

**HERRINGBONE KITCHENS**
www.herringbonekitchens.com
*Bespoke kitchens designed and handmade in Kent, England.*

**HOUSE CURIOUS**
www.housecurious.co.uk
*An online lifestyle boutique selling a trend-led selection of home decor.*

**HOUSE DOCTOR**
www.housedoctor.com
*Danish home accessories and furniture.*

**HYPNOS**
www.hypnosbeds.com
*Handcrafted beds and mattresses favoured by The Queen. And me.*

**JONATHAN ADLER**
www.jonathanadler.com
*Glamorous homeware from the eponymous American designer.*

**KOHR BY ARSALAN**
www.kohr.co.uk
*Islamabad-based founder/designer Arsalan collaborates with local artisans to create luxury furniture and home accessories.*

**MADE.COM**
www.made.com
*Contemporary furniture and homeware direct from the designers.*

**MATTHEW WILLIAMSON**
www.matthewwilliamson.com
*The fashion-turned-decor designer's fabulously vibrant interiors collection.*

**MUCK N BRASS**
www.mucknbrass.com
*'Luxecycled' vintage/retro
furniture and homewares.*

**OKA**
www.oka.com
*Luxury furniture and home
accessories.*

**OLIVER BONAS**
www.oliverbonas.com
*Colourful homeware, fashion
and gifts.*

**OSBORNE & LITTLE**
www.osborneandlittle.com
*Fine fabric and wallpaper designs.*

**PAD LIFESTYLE**
www.padlifestyle.com
*Homeware and fashion sourced
from established and new
designers worldwide.*

**PAINTHOUSE**
www.painthouse.co.uk
*Toxin-free, smell-free paint that
works on all surfaces.*

**PAPERCHASE**
www.paperchase.com
*Design-led stationery, cards
and seasonal decor.*

**PERRIN & ROWE**
www.perrinandrowe.co.uk
*Bathroom and kitchen brassware,
chinaware and accessories.*

**PINKSTER**
www.pinkstergin.com
*My favourite pink gin, infused
with raspberries.*

**PRINT CLUB LONDON**
www.printclublondon.com
*Limited-edition screenprints.*

**SANDBERG WALLPAPER**
www.sandbergwallpaper.com
*Swedish design company specializing
in wallpaper and home accessories.*

**SARA MILLER LONDON**
www.saramiller.london
*A colourful gold-embellished
collection of luxury homeware
and stationery.*

**SOFAS & STUFF**
www.sofasandstuff.com
*Handmade sofas and chairs,
upholstered in any fabric you choose.*

**SOHO HOME**
www.sohohome.com
*Homeware as seen in Soho House
members' clubs around the world.*

**TIMOROUS BEASTIES**
www.timorousbeasties.com
*Surreal and provocative wallpapers
and textiles.*

**TOPPS TILES**
www.toppstiles.co.uk
*Huge range of affordable tiles.*

**W.A.GREEN**
www.wagreen.co.uk
*A lifestyle store offering a mix of
high-end established brands and
hot new designers.*

**WEST ELM**
www.westelm.com and
www.westelm.co.uk
*Modern furniture, home accessories
and decor.*

# Picture Credits

# Index

# Acknowledgments

When I launched The Pink House (pinkhouse.co.uk) blog and @pinkhouseliving Instagram account three years ago, I hoped one day my digital brand would become a book. That *Pink House Living* has been published so soon after I launched my blog and business fills me with joy – and gratitude.

I'd like to start by thanking my agent, Jane Graham Maw, and the excellent team at Ryland Peters & Small – Cindy, Annabel, Toni and Leslie – who helped me create the book I'd been dreaming of. Thank you for trusting my rose-tinted vision.

This book wouldn't have been half as good – or half as much fun – without my great friend, the amazing photographer Susie Lowe. Susie, you're the only person who can motivate me to get up at 5am (to avoid direct sunlight), iron the sheets (can't have a crumpled bed) or sweep under the table (dusty Cheerios aren't aspirational). Thanks for being brilliant.

A special thank you to Alison Perry, Kate Faithfull-Williams and Deborah James for their sage mentoring and advice. And to stylist Antonia McKenzie for her creativity and hard work. I think we're all due another night out!

A massive thanks to The Pink House's loyal readers and followers across the world for your kind words, enthusiasm and sense of humour. You guys are the best – please keep sharing your pink pics on Instagram tagging @pinkhouseliving #pinkhouseliving.

Thank you to all my lovely, talented 'Pinkspiration' interviewees, and the wonderful brands that have supported me on this crazy pink journey. Also a big thank you to Kate Watson-Smyth (Mad About The House) and Kimberly Duran (Swoon Worthy), whose expertise and encouragement helped inspire The Pink House.

Finally, thanks to my family and friends, in particular the super-tolerant Pink House Husband and our gorgeous children, Oscar and Zac. You might not share my passion for pink, but I love you all the same.